Dear Jessie,
Enjoy this
in your quiet
time. Love,
Uncle Lee

Blue Mountain Arts®

Bestselling Titles

By Susan Polis Schutz:

To My Daughter, with Love, on the Important Things in Life

To My Son, with Love

I Love You

By Douglas Pagels:

100 Things to Always Remember... and One Thing to Never Forget

For You, Just Because You're Very Special to Me

To the One Person I Consider to Be My Soul Mate

Is It Time to Make a Change?

by Deanna Beisser

To the Love of My Life

by Donna Fargo

A Lifetime of Love ...Poems on the Passages of Life

by Leonard Nimoy

Anthologies:

Always Believe in Yourself and Your Dreams

For You, My Daughter

I Love You, Mom

I'm Glad You Are My Sister

Marriage Is a Promise of Love

May You Always Have an Angel by Your Side

Take Each Day One Step at a Time

Teaching and Learning Are Lifelong Journeys

There Is Greatness Within You, My Son

Think Positive Thoughts Every Day

To My Child

With God by Your Side ...You Never Have to Be Alone

True Wealth

Reflections on What Matters Most in Life
A Blue Mountain Arts® Collection

Edited by Gary Morris

Blue Mountain Press™
Boulder, Colorado

Library of Congress Control Number: 2003115938
ISBN: 0-88396-796-0 (hardcover) — ISBN: 0-88396-795-2 (trade paper)

ACKNOWLEDGMENTS appear on page 80.

Certain trademarks are used under license.
BLUE MOUNTAIN PRESS is registered in the U.S. Patent and Trademark Office.

Manufactured in China.
First Printing: 2004

 This book is printed on recycled paper.

This book is printed on fine quality, laid embossed, 80 lb. paper. This paper has been specially produced to be acid free (neutral pH) and contains no groundwood or unbleached pulp. It conforms with all the requirements of the American National Standards Institute, Inc., so as to ensure that this book will last and be enjoyed by future generations.

Blue Mountain Arts, Inc.

P.O. Box 4549, Boulder, Colorado 80306

Contents

If You Want True Wealth...
Remember What Is
Most Important

It's not having everything go right;
it's facing whatever goes wrong.
It's not being without fear;
it's having the determination
     to go on in spite of it.
It is not where you stand,
but the direction you're going in.
It's more than never having bad moments;
   it's knowing you are always
    bigger than the moment.
It's believing you have already
     been given everything
you need to handle life.

It's not being able to rid
    the world of all its injustices;
it's being able to rise above them.
It's the belief in your heart
    that there will always be
more good than bad in the world.
Remember to live just this one day
and not add tomorrow's troubles
    to today's load.
Remember that every day ends
and brings a new tomorrow
full of exciting new things.
Love what you do,
    do the best you can,
and always remember
    how much you are loved.

— Vickie M. Worsham

It's More than What
You Earn...

There is nothing that makes men rich and strong but that which they carry inside of them. Wealth is of the heart, not of the hand.

— John Milton

You are not here merely to make a living. You are here in order to enable the world to live more amply, with greater vision, with a finer spirit of hope and achievement. You are here to enrich the world, and you impoverish yourself if you forget the errand.

— Woodrow T. Wilson

If you put your nose to the grindstone rough
    And keep it down there long enough,
You'll soon forget there are such things
    As brooks that babble and birds that sing.
In time three things will your world compose:
    Just you and the stone and your poor old nose.

— Author Unknown

Barter

Life has loveliness to sell,
  All beautiful and splendid things,
Blue waves whitened on a cliff,
  Soaring fire that sways and sings
And children's faces looking up
Holding wonder like a cup.

Life has loveliness to sell,
  Music like a curve of gold,
Scent of pine trees in the rain,
  Eyes that love you, arms that hold,
And for your spirit's still delight,
Holy thoughts that star the night.

Spend all you have for loveliness,
  Buy it and never count the cost;
For one white singing hour of peace
  Count many a year of strife well lost,
And for a breath of ecstasy
Give all you have been, or could be.

— Sara Teasdale

Prosperity Is
a State of Mind

Being rich isn't about money. Being rich is a state
of mind. Some of us, no matter how much money we
have, will never have enough, never be free enough to
take time to stop and eat the heart of the watermelon....
Some people are rich without ever being more than a
paycheck ahead of the game.

— Harvey Mackay

There are two ways of being happy; we may either
diminish our wants or augment our means. Either will do,
the result is the same. And it is for each man to decide
for himself, and do that which happens to be the easiest.
If you are idle or sick or poor, however hard it may be
for you to diminish your wants, it will be harder to
augment your means. If you are active and prosperous
or young or in good health, it may be easier for you to
augment your means than to diminish your wants. But if
you are wise, you will do both at the same time, young
or old, rich or poor, sick or well. And if you are very
wise, you will do both in such a way as to augment the
general happiness of society.

— Benjamin Franklin

Money may buy the husk of things, but not the kernel. It brings you food but not appetite, medicine but not health, acquaintances but not friends, servants but not faithfulness, days of joy but not peace or happiness.

— Henrik Ibsen

Man cannot live by bread alone. The making of money, the accumulation of material power, is not all there is to living. Life is something more than these, and the man who misses this truth misses the greatest joy and satisfaction that can come into his life — service for others.

— Edward Bok

He is a wise man who does not grieve for the things which he has not, but rejoices for those which he has.

— Epictetus

The Best Things in Life Are Free

The best things in life are nearest: Breath in your nostrils, light in your eyes, flowers at your feet, duties at your hand, the path of right just before you. Then do not grasp at the stars, but do life's plain, common work as it comes, certain that daily duties and daily bread are the sweetest things in life.

— Robert Louis Stevenson

If you want to feel rich, just count all of the things you have that money can't buy.

— Author Unknown

Every morning you are handed twenty-four golden hours. They are some of the few things in this world that you get free of charge. If you had all the money in the world, you couldn't buy an extra hour. What will you do with this priceless treasure?

— Author Unknown

Our Greatest Wealth

We are born with two eyes in front because we must not always look behind, but see what lies ahead beyond ourselves.

We are born to have two ears — one left, one right — so we can hear both sides, collect both the compliments and criticisms, to see which are right.

We are born with a brain concealed in a skull; no matter how poor we are, we are still rich, for no one can steal what our brain contains, packing in more jewels and rings than you can imagine.

We are born with two eyes, two ears, but one mouth, for the mouth is a sharp weapon — it can hurt, flirt, and kill. Remember our motto: talk less, listen, and see more.

We are born with only one heart; deep in our ribs, it reminds us to appreciate and give love from deep within.

— Author Unknown

The Most Priceless Gifts
Come from Your Heart

The best thing to give to your enemy is forgiveness;
to an opponent, tolerance; to a friend, your heart; to
your child, a good example; to a father, deference;
to your mother, conduct that will make her proud of
you; to yourself, respect; to all men, charity.

— Francis Maitland Balfour

All of us can give friendship to those who need it;
loyalty to those who depend upon us; courtesy to all
those with whom we come in contact; kindness to
those whose paths may cross ours; understanding to
those whose views may not be exactly in accord with
our own opinions.

— Carl E. Holmes

The priceless gifts in life
are not the ones wrapped up
and given on special occasions,
but the gifts we give when
we give of ourselves.
It is the love we share.
It is the comfort we lend at times of need.
It is the moments we spend together
helping each other follow our dreams.
The most priceless gifts
are the understanding and caring
that come from the heart.
And each and every one of us
has these gifts to offer...
through the gift of ourselves.

— Ben Daniels

Your Life Is Valuable
to Everyone Else

The majority of us lead quiet, unheralded lives as we pass through this world. There will most likely be no ticker-tape parades for us, no monuments created in our honor. But that does not lessen our possible impact, for there are scores of people waiting for someone just like us to come along; people who will appreciate our compassion, our unique talents. Someone who will live a happier life merely because we took the time to share what we had to give. Too often we underestimate the power of a touch, a smile, a kind word, a listening ear, an honest compliment, or the smallest act of caring, all of which have a potential to turn a life around. It's overwhelming to consider the continuous opportunities there are to make our love felt.

— Leo Buscaglia

Act as if what you do makes a difference. It does.

— William James

You can't live a perfect day without doing something for someone who will never be able to repay you.

— John Wooden

If a man measures life by what others do for him, he is apt to be disappointed; but if he measures life by what he does for others, there is no time for despair. If he measures life by its accumulations, these usually fall short of his expectations, but if he measures life by the contribution which he has made to the sum of human happiness, his only disappointment is in not finding time to do all that his heart prompts him to do. Whether he spends his time trying to absorb from the world only to have the burden of life grow daily heavier, or spends his time in an effort to accomplish something of real value to the race, depends upon his ideal.

— William Jennings Bryan

True Wealth Is Found in...
Service to Others

After the verb "to Love," "to Help" is the most beautiful verb in the world.

— Bertha von Suttner

Doing good to others is not a duty. It is a joy, for it increases your own health and happiness.

— Zoroaster

If you have nothing else to do, look about you and see if there isn't something close at hand that you can improve! It may make you wealthy, though it is more likely that it will make you happy.

— George Matthew Adams

The sole meaning of life is to serve humanity.

— Leo Tolstoy

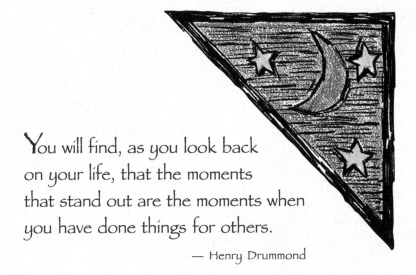

You will find, as you look back
on your life, that the moments
that stand out are the moments when
you have done things for others.

— Henry Drummond

Make it a rule... never to lie down at night without
being able to say, "I have made one human being at least
a little wiser, a little happier, or a little better this day."

— Charles Kingsley

I expect to pass through this world but once. Any good
thing, therefore, that I can do or any kindness I can
show to any fellow human being, let me do it now. Let me
not defer nor neglect it, for I shall not pass this way again.

— Etienne de Grellet

Nothing Is Worth
More than Friendship...

Without relationships, no matter how much wealth, fame, power, prestige, and seeming success by the standards and opinions of the world one has, happiness will constantly elude.

— Sidney Madwed

It's what each of us sows, and how, that gives to us character and prestige. Seeds of kindness, goodwill, and human understanding, planted in fertile soil, spring up into deathless friendships, big deeds of worth, and a memory that will not soon fade.

— George Matthew Adams

When two people join together as friends, it is truly one of life's greatest gifts. Friends stand beside each other, not in front or behind. They are two people joined in the soul, transcending all known bonds and life's limitations.

— Sharon Whyte

...and Family

The best feeling in this world
   is family.
From it, we draw love,
   friendship, moral support,
and the fulfillment of every
   special need within our hearts.
In a family, we are connected to
   an ever-present source
of sunny moments, smiles and laughter,
understanding and encouragement,
and hugs that help us grow
   in confidence
   all along life's path.
Wherever we are,
whatever we're doing,
whenever we really need to feel
   especially loved, befriended,
      supported, and cared for
         in the greatest way,
we can turn to family
and find the very best
   always waiting for us.

— Barbara J. Hall

Share Yourself with Those
You Love

Smile each day
for those you love.
Let them know by the
brightness of your face
that you are happy they're
in your life. Even if there
are times when you
argue and disagree.

Touch each day
those you love.
Hold them close, even if briefly.
The human touch is one of the
most comforting things in our
world, and one of the most reassuring.

Speak softly each day
to those you love.
Those whispers of intimacy
that tell them what you say
are important, but meant
for their ears and their ears only.

Muse quietly each day
on those you love.
Allow yourself to find those things
that you truly admire and respect
in that person. Forgetting, at least
for the moment, any of the negative.

Allow yourself to be vulnerable
to those you love.
It is a most frightening experience
to be without shields, but it can
also be the most wonderful thing in
the world to find another holds your
spirit carefully within their heart.

Believe that you deserve
those you love.
Your love is the most precious
gift that you can bestow on another
human. You deserve to be loved in return.
Without constraints. Without reserve.

Be honest
with those you love.
Let them know how important
they are in your life.
Take care that they never have to
guess at what you think and feel.
There may come a time when they
walk away... and then would you regret
not telling them? In all possible ways?

— Brenda Hager

The Lasting Value of
a Simple Life

To live content with small means; to seek elegance rather than luxury, and refinement rather than fashion; to be worthy, not respectable, and wealthy, not rich; to study hard, think quietly, talk gently, act frankly; to listen to stars and birds, to babes and sages, with open heart; to bear all cheerfully, do all bravely, await occasions, hurry never. In a word, to let the spiritual, unbidden, and unconscious grow up through the common. This is to be my symphony.

— William Ellery Channing

Simplicity is making the journey of this life with just baggage enough.

— Charles Dudley Warner

Where are all the people
who enjoyed simple things
who used to go out in the sunlight
and sing songs as they gardened
stopping and talking with
all the neighbors?
Where are all the people
who enjoyed life
who used to consider the home
the most important place to be
and who used to consider the family
the most important people to be with?
Times have changed most of these people
and urged them to seek the complicated
Yet it is only the very basic simple things
in life
that can make people truly
happy

— Susan Polis Schutz

The Art of
Taking Time to Live

To get the most out of life we must take time to live as well as to make a living. We must practice the art of filling our moments with enriching experiences that will give new meaning and depth to our lives.

We should take time for good books; time to absorb the thoughts of poets and philosophers, seers and prophets.

Time for music that washes away from the soul the dust of everyday life.

Time for friendships; time for talks by the fire and walks beneath the stars.

Time for laughter; time for letting go and filling the heart with mirth.

Time for travel; time for pilgrimage and festival, for shrine and exhibit, for rockbound coast and desert, mountain and plain.

Time for nature; time for flower gardens, trees, birds, and sunsets.

Time to love and be loved, for love is the greatest thing in the world.

Time for people; time for the interplay of personalities and the interchange of ideas.

Time for solitude; time to be quiet and alone and to look within.

Time to give of ourselves, our talents, abilities, devotions, and convictions, that we may contribute to the onward march of humanity.

Time for worship; time for opening our lives to God's infinite springs of vitality, that we may live more abundantly.

In all ways let us make our moments glow with life. Let us pray as did Matthew Arnold: "Calm, calm me more, nor let me die, before I have begun to live."

— Wilferd A. Peterson

To be rich in admiration and free from envy; to
rejoice greatly in the good of others; to love with
such generosity of heart that your love is still a dear
possession in absence. These are the gifts of fortune
which money cannot buy, and without which money
can buy nothing.

— Robert Louis Stevenson

Simplicity, simplicity, simplicity! I say let your
affairs be as one, two, three and to a hundred or
a thousand.... We are happy in proportion to the
things we can do without.

— Henry David Thoreau

What a man is contributes much more to his
happiness than what he has.... What a man is in himself,
what accompanies him when he is alone, what no one
can give him or take away, is obviously more essential
to him than everything he has in the way of possessions,
or even what he may be in the eyes of the world.

— Arthur Schopenhauer

It's not what you possess, but what you do with what you have.

— Thomas Carlyle

Infinite riches are all around you if you will open your mental eyes and behold the treasure house of infinity within you. There is a gold mine within you from which you can extract everything you need to live life gloriously, joyously, and abundantly.

— Joseph Murphy

Wealth is not found in our bank accounts, but in the treasury of feelings we share with friends and family. This truly can never be equaled or replaced by any amount of money.

— Mary E. Burkette

To find the universal elements enough; to find the air and the water exhilarating; to be refreshed by a morning walk or an evening saunter… to be thrilled by the stars at night; to be elated over a bird's nest or a wildflower in spring.

— John Burroughs

Keep a Balance in
Everything You Do

Imagine life as a game in which you are juggling five balls in the air. You name them — work, family, health, friends, and spirit — and you're keeping all of these in the air. You will soon understand that work is a rubber ball. If you drop it, it will bounce back. But the other four balls — family, health, friends, and spirit are made of glass. If you drop one of these, they will be irrevocably scuffed, marked, nicked, damaged, or even shattered. They will never be the same. You must understand that and strive for balance in your life.

— Brian Dyson

So many people walk around with a meaningless life. They seem half asleep, even when they're busy doing things they think are important. This is because they're chasing the wrong things. The way you get meaning into your life is to devote yourself to loving others, devote yourself to your community around you, and devote yourself to creating something that gives you purpose and meaning.

— Morrie Schwartz

We are all getting older every day, but we don't have to grow older every day. Taking time to daydream, visit a friend, watch your children grow, or just play in your garden is time well-spent. There is a rush to tomorrow by all of us. We are being prodded into the future by faster computers, shorter delivery times, and a general need to have it, do it, and see it all: NOW!

Take time today for yourself. Take time to breathe in life, all of it: its color, splendor, smells, tastes, and sounds. From the smallest, most insignificant event to the things you have taken for granted.

Tomorrow will be here before you know it. Today will be a distant memory before you realize it. We create our futures and memories in the present. Go through life today, conscious of your surroundings. Why not take a long weekend walking through nature? There are a lot of lessons that nature can teach us, if we will only carefully observe and listen.

Today is a gift of life. Live it with gratitude and don't let the sun set today without seeing it, hearing it, and enjoying it.

— Tim Connor

Cultivate a Sense
of Gratitude

Gratitude unlocks the fullness of life. It turns what we have into enough, and more. It turns denial into acceptance, chaos to order, confusion to clarity. It can turn a meal into a feast, a house into a home, a stranger into a friend. Gratitude makes sense of our past, brings peace for today, and creates a vision for tomorrow.

— Melody Beattie

Count your garden by the flowers,
Never by the leaves that fall;
Count your days by golden hours,
Don't remember clouds at all!

— John R. McCrillis

Be thankful for the smallest blessing, and you will deserve to receive greater. Value the least gifts no less than the greatest, and simple graces as especial favors. If you remember the dignity of the Giver, no gift will seem small or mean....

— Thomas à Kempis

Be grateful for the kindly friends that walk along your way;
Be grateful for the skies of blue that smile from day to day;
Be grateful for the health you own, the work you find to do,
For round about you there are men less fortunate than you.

Be grateful for the growing trees, the roses soon to bloom,
The tenderness of kindly hearts that shared your days of gloom;
Be grateful for the morning dew, the grass beneath your feet,
The soft caresses of your babes and all their laughter sweet.

Acquire the grateful habit, learn to see how blest you are,
How much there is to gladden life, how little life to mar!
And what if rain shall fall today and you with grief are sad;
Be grateful that you can recall the joys that you have had.

— Edgar A. Guest

Gratitude is a currency that we can mint for ourselves
and spend without fear of bankruptcy.

— Fred Dewitt Van Amburgh

How to Be Happy

1. Make up your mind to be happy.
   Learn to find pleasure in simple things.

2. Make the best of your circumstances.
   No one has everything, and everyone has
   something of sorrow intermingled with
   gladness of life. The trick is to make the
   laughter outweigh the tears.

3. Don't take yourself too seriously.
   Don't think that somehow you should be
   protected from misfortune that befalls
   other people.

4. You can't please everybody.
   Don't let criticism worry you.

5. Don't let your neighbor set your standards.
   Be yourself.

6. Do the things you enjoy doing, but stay out of debt.

7. Never borrow trouble.
   Imaginary things are harder to bear than real ones.

8. Since hate poisons the soul, do not cherish jealousy, enmity, grudges.
   Avoid people who make you unhappy.

9. Have many interests.
   If you can't travel, read about new places.

10. Don't hold postmortems.
    Don't spend your time brooding over sorrows or mistakes. Don't be one who never gets over things.

11. Do what you can for those less fortunate than yourself.

12. Keep busy at something.
    A busy person never has time to be unhappy.

— Robert Louis Stevenson

Spend Your Time Wisely

A day is well lived in which you have put a fine resolution into practice, achieved a definite purpose, done some worthy act of kindness, or rendered a noble service to others.

— Grenville Kleiser

Time is more valuable than money. You can get more money, but you cannot get more time.

— Jim Rohn

Know the true value of time; snatch, seize, and enjoy every moment of it. No idleness, no laziness, no procrastination; never put off till tomorrow what you can do today.

— Lord Chesterfield

Guard well your spare moments. They are like uncut diamonds. Discard them and their value will never be known. Improve them and they will become the brightest gems in a useful life.

— Ralph Waldo Emerson

Remember: A life well lived is simply a compilation of days well spent. So treasure the tremendous value of the moments right before your eyes. Reach out for the prizes you seek, and get a little closer to them with the setting of every sun.

Make *this one day* a journey of love and achievement, gently powered by all the benefits of understanding, commitment, and hope. Be healthy, happy, and continually rewarded for doing things that you know in your heart... are right.

May you discover every joy that wants to come true for you... on your precious journey through life.

— Douglas Pagels

Value What's Important

You can achieve wealth, fame, and power, but if there is no love in your heart, it all means very little. Your life can be filled with excitement and drama, but if it is not a life of integrity then it ends up getting you nowhere.

The fleeting, superficial things that the world makes out to be so terribly important are not that important after all. The things that truly matter are the things too often ignored.

Do those things over which you worry, fight, and argue really mean that much? The things that truly matter are the things you cannot lose. No person or circumstance can take away your love, your faith, your integrity, passion, determination, or wisdom. It pays to keep that in mind as you travel through each day.

For when you value and make use of what's truly important, all other things are surely within your reach.

— Ralph Marston

You Can Never Have
Too Much of This...

Freedom and honesty...
    to truly get to know yourself and what you want in life.
Joy and wonder...
    the kind you get from loving someone more deeply
    than you ever dreamed possible and the happiness
    of sharing life with them.
Strength and confidence...
    the kind that comes from those experiences that
    teach you that you can rely on yourself and you
    do have something to say about your destiny.
Courage and energy...
    to pursue the adventure of exploring your own
    dreams — big or small.
Tolerance, insight, and perspective...
    to see others as they are and let them be,
    along with the gentle openness to learn from them
    and apply what you can to your own life, while still
    maintaining the values that are right for you.
Peace and happiness...
    the kind that comes from knowing you are loved.

— Deeva D. Boleman

The Keys to Abundance

The great universe is filled with an abundance of all things, filled to overflowing. All there is, is in her, waiting only for the touch of the right forces to cast them forth.

— Ralph W. Trine

Abundance is our natural birthright and something we all have the right to experience. Abundance is much more than just having material success. It's the ability to ride the waves of abundant life. Are you ready to experience the waves or are you prepared only to watch others enjoy the ride? And if you catch a wave will you be dragged under? Abundance mentality is more than twinkly pretty pictures in your mind or warm and fuzzy feelings in your heart. It is a practice, whole body and whole-of-life. It's a skill that you refine. It is the way that you live.

— Michael Breen

True wealth is an emotion: it's a sense of absolute abundance. Our heritage alone makes us wealthy. We have the privilege of enjoying great works of art that we didn't paint, music we didn't compose, great educational institutions we didn't build. Feel the wealth of the nation's parks that you own. Know that you're a wealthy person now, and enjoy that wealth. Realize that this is a part of your abundance, and this feeling of gratitude will allow you to create even more.

— Anthony Robbins

An "abundance mentality" is more than having a positive mental attitude, although a positive mental attitude is very important. When you have a positive mental attitude, you look at how things can be done rather than why they can't be done. You believe that "where there's a will, there's a way." You look at possibilities and opportunities rather than obstacles and problems. This mindset is important for success in any endeavor.

An abundance mentality will take you beyond a positive mental attitude. It will eliminate small thinking and offset negative energy. It can mean the difference between success and failure, excellence and mediocrity, and prosperity and despair....

People with an abundance mentality believe there are enough resources available to accomplish their goals. They also believe that their success doesn't mean failure for others. On the contrary, the more successful they are, the more others are affected in a positive way....

Abundance starts in your mind. The more you think abundantly, the more abundance you can enjoy, the more success you will enjoy.

— Rex Houze

Build Your Life
on What's Truly
Important

Fill your life's treasure chest
    with the very best things:
hope and happiness shaped by love,
faith in finding your ultimate purpose,
strength for traveling in the
    right direction,
values that make your heart shine
    with kindness,
insight to see the difference
    between knowledge and wisdom,
and the maturity to choose true gifts
    over gold.
Fill your life's treasure chest
    with the very best things —
and make your days meaningful
    so your spirit can grow.

— Lisa L. Smith

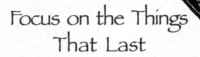

Focus on the Things That Last

Base your life on things that last. Money and fame are fleeting and temporal. So many of those things we chase after and place so much importance on don't give us the lasting satisfaction we thought they would. They are great for a while, but sooner or later they lose their luster. The new gadget we thought we needed last week has already been replaced by something better.

True wealth must not be defined by what you own or where you work. It is not something external; it comes from within and moves outward. It must be measured by how much you give of yourself to others and what you can do to make the ones you love happy. It's not how many friends you have, but how many you can trust your life with and who would be there with certainty if they were called on in an emergency. True wealth is how much love you have in your life, for it is the people in your life that really matter.

— Lori A. Heyd

Be Generous with Your Kind Words

Words can be the doorbell that gains us entry into a heart. They can light up a life through the windows of the soul. Words can bring rays of hope that can even create miracles when you say them to someone who needs them most.

Words can be our own security blanket that makes us feel safe from harm. They're the pillow where our dreams sleep and wait to come true. They are stored in the memory so they can be recalled, like a life raft that appears out of the blue.

Words can be the alarm clock to our psyche, our sleep enhancer, and wake-up call. They can shake us to our senses and move us to a different place. They're the candle that lights our fire to keep us from giving up, and they can save us in the midnight hour when we're about to lose the race.

Whether negative or positive, they're the secret to creation. They're life to those who say them; listen to your words today. Like a seed that becomes a flower, a word reproduces after its own kind. What are you calling into being by the words you choose to say?

Words can be the catalyst to change someone's life. Are you using your power to help someone along the way? Kindness takes so little effort, and words can mean so much, so let's all use our vocabulary to love someone today.

— Donna Fargo

Make Your Life
a Bountiful Garden

Accept the gift of life. All you can be is already within you. You are unique in every way; it's up to you to discover what lies inside you.

Trust that the power of life will bring you to your destination. Like a seed that is predestined to grow into a tree or flower, you are destined to bloom with all the blessings of life.

No matter what you are going through, make your life a garden.

Do whatever it takes to grow from seed to harvest: propagate love, prune illusions, weed out distractions. Remember that each garden is unique.

Like a rose, you do not bloom for your sake only. You also bloom for those who need to see your beauty or who seek serenity of spirit. Just by being the way you are, you give others the essence of your heart — you touch them with your influence. May your heart be like an open gate, inviting passersby to find refuge in your faith. May there always be a winding path of wisdom for you to stroll on through the garden of your life.

— Tanya P. Shubin

You're Richer than You Think...

If you spend most of your waking hours working at something you enjoy.

If you never waste a minute comparing yourself to anyone else.

If you always do your best, making the most of what you have at this moment in time.

If you never worry about tomorrow — knowing that when you spend today as best as you can, you will change your future for the better.

If you treat everyone around you with respect and understanding — knowing that when you invest yourself in other lives, you will be greatly rewarded down the road.

If you have a place to come home to at the end of the day that feels like a sanctuary for your spirit and a garden for your soul.

If you can look back on decisions you've made with a confident heart, a clear conscience, and the understanding that for the most part you'd make the same choices all over again.

If you have friends who are always glad to see you —
and who are there to call on anytime.
If you wake up every morning looking forward to whatever
the day ahead might bring — knowing that difficulties are
only temporary, but the good things last forever.
If you have a dream that draws out the best in you —
one that spurs your greatest efforts, and influences
you to continue improving your skills on a daily basis.
If you gaze in wonder at the world and find beauty in
every setting — whether it's the sun reflecting off
snow-capped mountain peaks or a wildflower sprouting
up among the weeds in a vacant downtown city lot.
If you know how lucky you are to be in the world at
this particular place and time, and to have so much to
be grateful for...

If you are blessed with even a few of these — the
greatest gifts in life — then you truly are richer than
you think.

— Jon Peyton

There Are Things Money Can't Buy

The things money can't buy would make
a long list... here are some of them:

Money can't buy the ability to think...
thought makes us what we are.
Money can't buy friendship...
friendship must be deserved.
Money can't buy a clear conscience...
honesty is the price tag.
Money can't buy the glow of good
health... right living is the secret.
Money can't buy happiness...
happiness is a mental attitude.

Money can't buy sunsets, singing birds, the stars, moonlight, the music of the wind in the trees... the best things in life are free.

Money can't buy peace of mind... inner peace is the result of a constructive philosophy of life.

Money can't buy love... love comes when we give ourselves away to others.

Money can't buy the freedom to choose... choice controls our destiny.

Money can't buy character... character is what we are when we are alone with ourselves in the dark.

Continue the list yourself. You'll agree that among the things money can't buy are the most valuable treasures life has to offer us.

— Wilferd A. Peterson

If You Want to Feel like a Million Dollars... Have Some Fun Today!

Sometimes we get so caught up in the day-to-day minutiae of our lives, we forget to come up for air, to take a deep breath, and to appreciate the sunrise and sunset.

No matter what is going on in your life, take time for pleasure today, whether it's a few minutes or a few hours. You will be renewed and refreshed if you set aside special time just for you, and you'll ultimately become more productive.

Do something fun today — read a romance novel, slide down a slide, swim, jump, laugh. Hang out with a good friend. Relish time alone.

We often forget the joy found in a brisk walk, a hot cup of cocoa, or a hilarious movie seen with a close friend.

Whatever you choose to do, remember to have fun today — to smile, to laugh, to touch someone else's life in a positive way. Say thank you for this day... and then enjoy it!

You deserve to have fun today... and every day!

— Donna Gephart

Take a Little Time
for What Really Matters

Take a little time for yourself, to rediscover who
you are, what you like, and where your passions lie.
Slow down your pace so you can reflect on what
you really want in your life, what you want to give
to your life, and what your life truly means to you.

Take a little time for your family, to be with your
loved ones. They are always waiting for you to
share a piece of your world with them.

Take a little time for your friends, to laugh and joke
and have easy conversations — to just hang out
and be together.

Take a little time to relax and pamper yourself. Whether it's doing something you like or doing nothing at all, enjoy the beautiful simplicities that life has to offer.

Take a little time to learn something new, to get involved in something exciting that sparks your enthusiasm and incites your passion.

Take a little time to meet new people, to listen to children and elders. They all have their words of wisdom.

Take a little time. You deserve it for yourself and for all those who love you.

— Debbie Burton-Peddle

Ten Ways to Enrich
Each of Your Days

1. If each day is too short for all the wonderful things you want to do, don't be frustrated.

2. Be thankful... that your wish list is so full.

3. With the beginning of each sunrise, think to yourself: "Here's a brand-new day coming into my life. I can't wait to see how we'll get along! I wonder what's in store for us? What an adventure... spending time with a day I've never met before!"

4. Be open to the possibilities.

5. Count your blessings. Each one is so valuable and they're the best treasures you've got. And while you're counting the big things, be sure to include the smaller ones, too.

6. A little added to a little... adds up to a lot.

7. Everyone's life is lived somewhere between their aspirations and their limitations. Successful people have limitations like everyone else, and setbacks that are hard to ignore. But they offset them with efforts and aspirations... that absolutely soar.

8. Try hard and dream big.

9. If you think of your life as a story that gradually unfolds, you will embrace the changes and more fully appreciate the moments. You will know how natural it is for new chapters to begin and for the characters and events to surprise you every now and then. You will cherish your heroes and overcome your foes. And you can still have a beautiful story even if it hasn't been great all along. Make the best of everything, and...

10. Always enjoy reading the page you're on!

— Douglas Pagels

The Best Way to "Get Ahead..."

One of the most effective ways to create a happier, less stressed, and more balanced life is to remember that there is far more to life than winning and losing... when we look back on our lives from our deathbeds — a year from now, five years, ten, twenty, fifty, or whatever — it's almost certain that the most important aspects will not have been our ability to dominate others, collect achievements, win contests, and beat out our competition.

Instead, the things that will seem most important will be the quality of our lives. We will measure the success of our lives by the type of relationships we had with ourselves and with others. We will reflect upon our children, spouse or girlfriend, relatives, friends, colleagues, and other important people in our lives. We will value qualities such as compassion, patience, generosity, and kindness. We will remember the touching moments and heartwarming experiences.

— Richard Carlson

The mark of a successful man is one that has spent an entire day on the bank of a river without feeling guilty about it.

— Author Unknown

Try an experiment in your life: Slow down your mind and your actions. While driving on the freeway, slow down one or two miles an hour. You will get there faster. While saying good night or good morning to your loved ones, take just a little longer. You will find your relationships improve. When you give a hug, make it last a little longer. When working, take a little extra time. Your satisfaction and production will skyrocket. You will see immediate results and improvement in the quality of your life.

— Milton Willis and Michael Willis

Don't run through life so fast that you forget not only where you've been but also where you're going. Life is not a race, but a journey to be savored each step of the way.

— Nancye Sims

Inner Fulfillment
Is Life's Greatest Reward

Accomplishments are the main barometer the world uses to measure success: breaking records, amassing fortunes, being the first to do something, or changing current mind-sets all qualify. Being the best at something, conquering, curing, breaking through some barrier all deem one eligible to enter the hallowed halls of success.

Fulfillment, however, is something quite different. Fulfillment is a feeling that comes from within your soul that radiates through your being. It is the feeling of deep satisfaction and contentment you experience at the end of the day when you lie in bed before drifting off into sleep, knowing in your heart and your bones that you have met or exceeded your expectations of yourself. To be fulfilled means to be "filled full" with a sense of well-being.

When your own sense of well-being and the external symbols of accomplishment converge, then you have achieved "success." One without the other is like a candle without a match: Each can exist separately, but when used together, the resulting flame creates a miraculous glow.

— Chérie Carter-Scott

Work Toward Happiness

To be without desire is to be content. But contentment is not happiness. And in contentment there is no progress. Happiness is to desire something, to work for it, and to obtain at least a part of it. In the pursuit of beloved labor the busy days pass cheerfully employed, and the still nights in peaceful sleep. For labor born of desire is not drudgery, but manly play. Success brings hope, hope inspires fresh desire, and desire gives zest to life and joy to labor. This is true whether your days be spent in the palaces of the powerful or in some little green by-way of the world. Therefore, while yet you have the strength, cherish a desire to do some useful work in your little corner of the world, and have the steadfastness to labor. For this is the way to the happy life; with health and endearing ties, it is the way to the glorious life.

— Max Ehrmann

Love What You Do
for a Living

When you work for the thing you believe in,
you're rich though the whole way is rough.
But work that is simply for money
will never quite pay you enough.

— Rebecca McCann

We are not sent into this world to do anything into
which we cannot put our whole hearts. We have certain
things to do for our bread, and that is to be done
strenuously; other work to do for our delight, and that
is to be done heartily; neither is to be done by halves
or shifts, but with a will, and what is not worth this
effort is not to be done at all.

— John Ruskin

A man who does a little more work than he's asked to —
who takes a little more care than he's expected to —
who puts the small details on an equal footing with the
more important one — he's the man who is going to
make a success of his job. Each little thing done better
is the thin end of the wedge into something bigger.

— Author Unknown

We find greatest joy not in getting, but in expressing
what we are.... Men do not really live for honors or for
pay; their gladness is not the taking and holding, but in
doing, the striving, the building, the living. It is a higher
joy to teach than to be taught. It is good to get justice,
but better to do it; fun to have things, but more to make
them. The happy man is he who lives the life of love, not
for the honors it may bring, but for the life itself.

— R. J. Baughan

Get happiness out of your work or you may never
know what happiness is.

— Elbert Hubbard

What Is <u>Real</u> Success?

Everyone wants success, and yet they often don't
know when they have it.

For most, it is the maddening chase toward a better
way of life or more of something. More fame, power,
recognition, money, or
material stuff.
For some, it is the understanding of a loving partner,
the love of their child, or the people that they can
count on when life throws them a curve.

I am coming to believe that success is not more
material wealth, but peace, happiness, contentment, and love.

Most of all love.

Real success is not to be sought after in the outer world, but discovered in your inner world. I am not condemning the stuff of life. We all want the things that life offers.

But we don't need as much
as we think we do.

Sooner or later you will discover that real success is to be found in loving relationships. With your family, friends, strangers, and anyone who crosses your path. It is kindness shared, support given and received, listening, giving, and caring.

These will endure while your car rusts, your toys break, and you tire of the temporary gratifications that bring you what you think is real.

What matters is people.

What lasts is love. What counts are true friends, and if you treasure these you can count yourself a success.

— Tim Connor

The first wealth is health.

— Ralph Waldo Emerson

There's a lot of people in this world who spend so much time watching their health that they haven't the time to enjoy it.

— Josh Billings

He who enjoys good health is rich, though he knows it not.

— Italian Proverb

He who has health has hope; and he who has hope has everything.

— Arabian Proverb

The Coin

Into my heart's treasury
    I slipped a coin
That time cannot take
    Nor a thief purloin,
Oh, better than the minting
    Of a gold-crowned king
Is the safe-kept memory
    Of a lovely thing.

— Sara Teasdale

You are told a lot about your education, but some beautiful, sacred memory, preserved since childhood, is perhaps the best education of all. If a man carries many such memories into life with him, he is saved for the rest of his days. And even if only one good memory is left in our hearts, it may also be the instrument of our salvation one day.

— Fyodor Dostoyevski

As Long as You
Have Today...
You Have Everything

You may not know
   what tomorrow has in store,
but since you have today...
use the time for all the good
   you can do.

May you take this opportunity
   to live as best you can
and give everything you have
   to the special reasons
that make your life meaningful.
Remember to be thankful in a way
that sends a message to
   your fellow human beings —
offering help when it is needed,
giving before you're asked,
and sharing most willingly.

May you always appreciate what you have,
    especially what matters most:
the love of family and friends
and the liberty to love them back.
May the smiles, hugs, and happy moments
    shared together
make special memories for you
to save within your heart.
Be thankful for today and give it
    everything you have —
so that when tomorrow comes
    it will be worth the wait.

— Barbara J. Hall

Find Time to Enjoy
Your Life

Rest is not idleness, and to lie sometimes on the grass under trees on a summer's day, listening to the murmur of the water, or watching the clouds float across the sky, is by no means a waste of time.

— Sir John Lubbock

Take life too seriously, and what is it worth? If the morning wakes us to no new joys, if the evening brings us not the hope of new pleasures, is it worthwhile to dress and undress? Does the sun shine on me today that I may reflect on yesterday? That I may endeavor to foresee and to control what can neither be foreseen nor controlled — the destiny of tomorrow?

— Johann Wolfgang von Goethe

Loosen Up!

To desire success is a splendid thing, but to pursue success too tensely is to make certain of missing it. There is an attitude of mind which may be compared to a clenched fist, a knitted brow, and set teeth; and this attitude cannot bring success.

The carefree attitude of approach in any endeavor is a shortcut to success. In music, in sport, in study, in business life, many people fail, or advance very slowly, because *they make hard work of it.* They would succeed beyond their wildest expectations if they would treat it as fun.

Treat your work as fun. Regard the difficulties as part of the game, laugh off the annoyances, and the whole picture will change for the better, and stay changed. This, of course, is the real difference between work and play....

Take it easy. *Loosen up!*

— Emmet Fox

Invest Yourself

The times when you experience the highest level of fulfillment are the times when you give the most of yourself. The moments that are most meaningful are the moments into which you invest your effort, your energy, and your commitment.

If you do just enough to get by, that's precisely what will happen — you'll just get by. Yet when you truly invest yourself in life, with your time and work and attention, the dividends will be rich indeed.

It is your great fortune to be alive and living, aware and capable on this day that is filled with endless possibilities. You can squander that fortune or you can choose to expand and enlarge it even further.

The best that life has to offer cannot be bought with money. It can only be earned with your time, your effort, your attention and commitment.

Accomplishment and fulfillment cannot be purchased off the shelf. They come as a result of what you're willing to give.

Invest the best of yourself in this day, in this moment, in the great experience of living. It's an investment that will continue to pay increasingly valuable returns.

— Ralph Marston

I will not die an unlived life.
I will not live in fear of falling
or catching fire.
I choose to inhabit my days,
to allow my living to open me,
to make me less afraid,
more accessible;
to loosen my heart
until it becomes a wing,
a torch, a promise.
I choose to risk my significance,
to live so that which comes to me as seed
goes to the next as blossom,
and that which comes to me as blossom,
goes on as fruit.

— Dawna Markova

A Positive Attitude Is
Your Greatest Asset

Your living is determined not so much by
what life brings to you as by the attitude
you bring to life; not so much by what
happens to you as by the way your mind
looks at what happens.

Circumstances and situations do color life,
but you have been given the mind
to choose what the color will be.

— John Homer Miller

Enthusiasm is the greatest asset in the world.
It beats money, power, and influence.

— Henry Chester

Always think on the bright side — no
matter what life brings to your day. You'll
gain a treasure within your soul that no
worry or hardship can ever take away.

— Isaac Purcell

Go forward with your shoulders back, your head high, and with a smile. With your enthusiastic spirit, perseverance, and integrity of character, put your intelligence, talents, and passion into action.

Never let setbacks excuse you from trying again. It often takes many attempts to be a success.

Never let negative people influence you or direct what you do. Always face forward and see your whole life shining bright for you. Never let go of your character, ideals, or activism for the good of this world.

Never let go of the passions that inspire you, guide you, and always smile on you. These passions will lead you to reach your fullest potential. Hold on to them and they will keep you honest, caring, kind, and generous with the finest gifts your heart can give.

— Jacqueline Schiff

It's More than
Just the Money...

It is good to have money and the things that money can buy, but it's good too, to check up once in a while and make sure you haven't lost the things money can't buy.

— George Horace Lorimer

Ordinary riches can be stolen... real riches cannot. In your soul are infinitely precious things that cannot be taken from you.

— Oscar Wilde

Money isn't the most important thing to save. It is the least. Better to save your self-respect, your honor, your individual independence, your pride in being, and your health. These, and many more, are far better than gold.

— George Matthew Adams

Encouragement When It's Hard to Make Ends Meet...

*"Just about the time you think
you can make both ends meet...
somebody moves the ends."*

— Anonymous

There's a lot of truth to that,
isn't there? But there's also hope.
Because the harder you work at doing the
right things, the more the rewards
will come your way. The financial side
of things will get brighter. But while
the days go by, don't lose sight of the
things that are really important.

There are so many lessons we learn through
the years, and when it comes to things
like worth and value and what we truly
treasure, life is kind of funny:

Riches come in many forms —
and most of them have absolutely
nothing to do... with money.

— Carey Martin

How to Be Rich
(in All the Ways that Matter Most)

Always take time for...

Big smiles. Sunday mornings. Long walks. Warm appreciation. Precious memories. Things that bring a sense of joy to your heart. Staying in touch... with the people who will always mean so much.

Find a way to...

Be good to yourself (really good.) Build the bridges that will take you everywhere you've ever wanted to go. Write out your own definition of success, and then do your absolute best to make that story come true. Get closer and closer to the summit of every mountain you've ever wanted to climb. Make the most... of your moment... of this moment in time.

Make plans to…

Slow down the days. Find your perfect
pace. Be strong enough. Be gentle
enough. Reap the sweet rewards that will
come from all the good things you do and all the
great things you give. Keep things in perspective.

Remember to…

Invest wisely in the best riches of all. Share invaluable
words over warm cups in quiet places. Treasure time
spent in heart-to-heart conversations. Laugh a lot.
Work it all out. Move ahead of every worry. Move
beyond any sorrows. Have yourself a wealth of
beautiful tomorrows.

And (last, but not least)
never underestimate
the power of…

Friendship. Family. Chocolate.
And love.

— Douglas Pagels